Nirala Series

IN THE CITY OF PARTRIDGES

Highly acclaimed Hindi poet **Jagdish Chaturvedi** was born in Gwalior in 1933. He is known for the literary movement "Akavita" (Anti-Poetry) which aspired to change the face of contemporary Indian poetry. In a literary career spanning over more than five decades Chaturvedi has to his credit ten short story collections, one novel, two dramas, four books of criticism, four anthologies of translations and a Collected Works, *Jagdish Chaturvedi Rachnavali* in six volumes. His most noted poetry books include *Itihashanta* (1970), *Surya Putra,* (1975) *Doobte Itihas Ka Gavaha* (1980), *Kahin Kuch Kuredta Hai Mujhe* and *Connaught Place,* a novel centered on the repressive political scenario during Emergency Era in India. He has edited a number of anthologies and magazines including *Akavita* and *Bhasha.* His works have been translated into English, French, Serbo-Croatian, Korean, Nepali, Arabic and several Indian languages.

Widely traveled poet, Chaturvedi has received several prestigious awards and honors including *Padma Shree.*

Currently, he lives in New Delhi.

[illegible] Series

THE CRY OF PARTRIDGES

Highly acclaimed Hindi poet Jagdish Chaturvedi was born in [illegible] in 1933. He is known for the literary movement "Akavita" (Anti-Poetry) which aspired to change the face of contemporary Indian poetry. In a literary career spanning over more than five decades, Chaturvedi has to his credit ten short story collections, one novel, two dramas, four books of criticism, four anthologies of translations and a Collected Works, Jagdish Chaturvedi Rachnavali in six volumes. His most noted poetry books include [illegible] (1962), [illegible] (197[illegible]), [illegible] (1980), [illegible] The Muse and Company, The Place, a novel centered on the repressive political scenario during Emergency in India. He has edited a number of anthologies and magazines including Akavita and Bhasha. His works have been translated into English, French, Serbo-Croatian, Korean, Nepali, Assamese and several Indian languages.

Widely travelled poet, Chaturvedi has received several prestigious awards and honours including Padma Shri.

Currently he lives in New Delhi.

In the City of Partridges

Jagdish Chaturvedi

Translated from the Hindi

Nirala

Nirala Publications
96 B, Krishan Kunj Colony,
Laxmi Nagar, Delhi-110092
nirala32@hotmail.com

First Edition 2004

ISBN-81-85693-99-4

Cover Painting : K. Khosa

Distributed in Nepal by
White Lotus Book Shop,
Hanumansthan, Kupondole
Kathmandu, Nepal
whitelotusbookshop@hotmail.com

Printed at
H.S. Printers
New Delhi

Editorial Note

Jagdish Chturvedi is most discussed modern Hindi poet.

City of Partridges is a thundering collection of poems raging with notes of protest, dissent and fury against the sham, hypocritical norms and taboos that dominate the value system of contemporary India.

This first collection of Chatuvedi's poems in English translation includes not just fresh poems written lately but also controversial "Akavita" movement poems composed in the seventies and eighties.

And today he is a king in the city of partridges
His brain is locked in a tunnel
His shoulders and heart with the foxes
Have left the city.

Here in this collection one comes across a rare rage, " an anguished crusade against the rot", that has today become bedrock of modern Hindi literature. Here one encounters a city of stones where "culture vomits loads of lice, beetles and otters", where in a desolate land "flabby females" deliver babes to impotent husbands and the Poet is a Brahma ready to 'luxuriate in the flesh of "a poisonous generation."

And poetry scribbled by a few maniacs comes only through a cruel path to trouble the sleep of posh partridges.

And writing my name
in black blood of the corpse
on the last page of history
I throw that carcass of a woman
over in the ruins

-Yuyutsu RD Sharma,
General Editor, *Nirala Series*

Contents

IN THE CITY OF PARTRIDGES

Identity

How broken is this four legged animal ?

Incapacitated even to crawl
Films have enshrouded the eyes
Scorpion-trees have grown on cheeks
Whatever he sights, transforms into broken wings
Of a green butterfly.

His breast neighs like a horse
He cannot breathe but is stifled
Pain of swollen stomach and broken spine
Falls out everywhere like vomit
It constantly turns, a fly jumps up
over the vomit.

There are only some squalid, unskulled hair
Dust-eaten cannisters

Off-and-on yawns the animal
And whisk away into air--green
yellow and onion pewed worms.

There in the forest an aged bear runs
With a feel the woodman has discovered
his cave shut up for years.

Now to be unshut with a signpost
Of a blue mark of defeathered pigeon!

(Tr. Manohar Bandopadhyay)

Distortion

The sprawl of thirty-five years
marched past my shadow,
slaves in livery
riding high as Neros.

Onto the roof of the sky
the sun straggled up
and then said good-bye.
A few desperate blokes
in a conspiracy of lust and crime
kept me company
but wherever the street turned
they whistled past me
nonchalant, into blind alleys.

From History's long nose
were tied so many pennants
that it became a headache
which of them I should tear off,
to hang on the stirrups of my
ship of the desert.

Hands shrivel up,
all freckled my chin,
below the scar of the left temple -
on cheeks - are hollows like hell-holes:
the nasty wound that never heals,
Termites merrily eat away the breast.

Nothing I got
from the marionettes of rage
for the coin of love
only fading images

of hurried copulation
upon the jagged gravel
of a dead park,
and cindery embraces in musty bylanes.
while the piercing wind howled,
in the wobbling eyes
insects yellow, green crawling
that gave abortions, illegitimate children
or greenish-ripe fruits.

In vain I tried to sleep
the long nights,
for years a hideous python
in the very evening bites off
my cocoon of sleep.
As pain clatters down inside
the zenith of my eye
in forests and forests of reed
rattles down inside
mauling the body
with its piercing venom.
The echoes I remember
turn into black abyss,
I try to remember my childhood
a putrescent-old vulture
stands before me.
I forgot
the haunted ruins of Shivpuri
green dales of Malwa
the necromancers of Ujjain
orchards of orange,
in the sultry heat of Gwalior
the incendiarisms that I indulged in
though no house was on fire
neither any palace crumbled.

Everything went down
the dark alley of time,
now only the dust over the body
the hurting heat,
plague-blotches,
and the flayed skin.

Much time wasted
searching friends that were found never,
and those I found
shrugged me off
probably I too was callous.
My kin
taught me to pose
though the suffocation
oozed out of the carcass.

I scratched all my hair out
the scorched sun is tied to my head
from the last century.
Bound head to foot
I have been thrown into
a toppling house in roaring flames
a millennium I roam over this blessed country,
a stranger in deadly fear
none is there to call me dear
none shouts from behind
and asks for health
nor greets.
Often I think to hide me
in some damp garret
on destination unknown,
to turn an old mariner
in a creaking ship,

or bash the rectitude
of `J' in my name
or those who in recognition
look at me
neither should I nod back
and break in sweet greetings.

I want to live
in this murky-city
a weird demon
the last Machiavelli,
gnawing his own entrails.

(Tr.: Ashit Chakraborty)

Assassination of History

A horseman swiftly passed through
the fourteen thousand gorillas.

He triggered off the gun at the shoulders of culture
and spurting out at my shoulders the
burnt gas from the hot barrel
he loosened his thighs on the saddle.

Having pasted the face of a clown on
the shoulders of history
I stuffed all devoted wives into cells
Having bathed the piggish husbands in
hot water--tied them to the hooves of horses
for a general massacre.

Every inch of the town was
drowned in wails and cries
Tear-gas shells were exploded in
the innocent faces of children.
The beautiful young women were tied
to the tyres
and the cars raced on the burning
coaltar roads.

Setting the factories on fire
mechanic made the bonfire
and in place of smoke faces of
the clowns were poured out of chimneys.

Over a fire forced out from the naval
of women the century was to be roasted.

On a colossal rock there cracked an

egg in the image of Shiva
and began to devour the thighs and
the cities and the naked women.

In an attempt to be pasted
like a bold picture on some new era
burning the brows of my eyes I thrust
them in an oven.
Scratching at the fluffy hair on the
breasts of my beloved
lifted up the whole sky and threw it over on my left.

Joining a pack of dogs
I barked continuously.

I don't find any difference between
mother and sister, wife and mistress,
vamps look like wives.
In fear and trembling
the hand slips towards the thighs of some
naked woman.

In a river of burning lava
darting like a kite
Discarding history I do insert
myself in that privacy at white heat.

Picking embryos from the streets I
pack them in tins
hide them
under the sleeve of the jacket dripping blood.

I jump down the road
to give a mixed taste of whip and hooves
of the horse

to a young woman roaming about some
anonymous ruins.

And out of crumbling temples, clothes
and cathedrals
in a valley going to pieces
I drag a hand topped off
a fresh corpse
and I am absorbed in copulation
with that trembling corpse.

The sky whirls and scream the damp winds
Setting seventeen gorilla--cities on fire
Bearing the Venus of history on my shoulders
I climb up a mound of the dead.

And writing my name
in black blood of the corpse
on the last page of history
I throw that carcass of a woman
over in the ruins.

(Tr.: Ratan Chauhan)

In the City of Partridges

A city lies under his coat and another under his arms
Under his feet are hidden towns, flowers, valleys and
harvests.
Biting chill of January embraces his neck like an ostrich
The body has only a feeling of thin fingers
Weapons move away
And a magnetic rope is tied in his arms.

On way to office some pigeons meet
His bloody hands shiver
Fists clench
And an alertcat out of his pocket hunts them.

Recollecting hunting-grounds he is reminded of
Niagara falls or Bhadiya Kund seen in childhood
He moves fast
without caring for a group of kites, he moves towards a
bus
And anguish lies beside him like a camel
A rain does not disturb him of its water drops, shows
face of the broken shoe.

He believes
Water is to his liking in summer, not in winter
A common man links it up; with ration shop but he with
boredom

Boredom licked the soles of his feet in childhood
The more he tried to get rid of it, the more it licked like a
leech
Moss filled in his fragments of brain, light of eyes
and snaky holes of ribs.

Every where he ran fastest to get rid of the leech
At last he found
That leech was another name for attraction.
And all attractions he knows, are jungle-spider's nets
and to get rid of it is a must.

To avoid attraction he settled in a tunnel
A group of white-ants welcomed him
and he ran out of the tunnel.

While running his brain divorced his head
He did not try to get it back
He felt that brain had no place in this city
He would live lovely, lazy like a jar.

But his chest smouldered like an earthquake
On his left a bullet struck and a stream moved.
He discarded his brain, could't give up the beating of the heart.

With the sound like, minute-of-watch he spent years
Kept hunting foxes
Kept digging squirrel's hollow-homes
Kept drying his hair and kept making stories.

Getting bored one day he changed himself completely
Fixed eyes in place of mouth, thighs on chest like a cross
Seeing his ferocious state the foxes ran away
Cities come into being in jungles
Only partridges were left in the city.

And to-day he is a king in the city of partridges
His brain is locked in a tunnel
His shoulders and heart with the foxes
Have left the city.

(Tr.: Kedar Nath Komal)

Self-Condemnation

Exile me oh my country-
I have lived the life of matricide whole three generations
in ghastly terror,
I drove with my murderous fangs.

Craving for a mass murder
A guerilla platoon
I commanded to take position in the highway itself.

My heavy hand alone was capable
of doing the impossible tasks
of spreading poison gas in pure air
and I spread it.

Hang me oh my country-
I deluded the faithful friends,
took limbs apart from the children
In a series of historical crimes,
I did spend my days and years
And now I spend my nights
upon a bed of eyeless skulls.

Often I caressed the petal--touch breasts of women
No pleasure I felt,
So I bit them off in a mouthful like a giant hairy ape
And then spat upon dead streets of a city dead.

I see that hand that did not forgive
blazing in the dark.
The executioners who would impale me on the stakes
just now disappeared
behind the turn of the street
one of them carried a mace in his fist

The other a heavy tomahawk.

Cut me into two, oh love that will come after me
Lying on flowers and smell of air
I vomitted purified adulteries in dull parks.

To liquidate my whole family
A pest of the arsenal itself
I stored lovingly into the underground room.

My criminal hand even does not know
when it will push the button for the dark tunnel
to explode in a deafening blast.

Death, love, desire, deception
I have cooled off
And all these are now strangely strange to me.

Wife or love
women or a hussy-
with none I like sleeping now.
For me the band in the bar and the harmonium
at the house of a prostitute
All sound the same.

Tie me with a stone
And throw me away my country!

I have swallowed a stone into my body
Ane having lost all taste for any facts
I now live wrapped in the garb
of my inhuman diginity.

(Td.: Ashit Chakraborty)

Safe and Sound

Imprisoned in the coils of a serpent huge
lies the total town.
And I'm being crushed
by a gruesome ocean-churn.

Culture vomits loads of lice, beetles and otters.
Bearing leprous wounds on naked lips
humanity keeps shrieking time and again.
With bodies blued and swollen breasts
women fight shy of impregnation.

Unsafe human pups, pussies and kids,
All keep groaning in a rounded cage.
Rendered impotent are those who
stab and rape.
Fearful doctors in hospitals put goggles on
and women have ceased to menstruate.

Inserted in the blind highways
is a tube in this desolate land
where flabby females deliver babes
and impotent fathers return beating drums.

Bound in a poison-fuming tail
people curse monkeys,
tie amulets on arms of their brides
after first administering sleeping pills.
Not flesh, rubber pads are nailed
on wound-infested rounds,
and half the town moves about
with tubercular germs in intestines.

Lifeless are germ-filled breasts and aching veins

People shudder recognition.
Locked in container, they read *Gita* or *Kamasutra* *
and this land is converted into a rent-free inn.

In name of religion remain
a few mangled breasts.
And the entire century is busy dancing
assiduous attendance on them.
And so is each of my fellow countrymen,
All, all,
same me.

(Tr.: Manmohan Thakore)

* Ancient sanskrit text of Sexology.

Statement Made by one who is Lone and Desolate

In the country fallen into a daze and
in the cities intoxicated, there hobbles a
man lone and desolate.... the eyes hang
out dislocated from the sockets, the jungles
of thought disappear, a tune on sitar
is played somewhere in the distance, people howl,
they do not listen to Alla Rakkha's tabla
or Shipley's Guitar.

The white sunshine descends from the
cornice and is lost in the red-gravelled road.
Strike means another dull day,
a release from the news headlines and odd jobs of work.

A kite descends noiselessly from the sky and
is lost in a thick jungle of pine.
Nobody stretches his limbs,
Whether he is a wrestler or a woman hot
like cracking sunshine. Pain settles in
every joint. Sick, sad and disappointed,
all-invalids
exhaling black smoke of despair.

In the midst of sky there occurs a death
unconceivable
and blood drips in farm yards--rains,
hailstones and pestilence-many a
La Peste are shaped by Camus
and in a desperate struggle to save
mankind metamorphosed in rats.

There rises the number of rats in cities,
on maps, in offices, in gutters, at news
papers' and among the leaders.

The country--an old limping invalid.
Patriotism is a chant sung by a degenerate.
Some nerve in the brain aches and
there crops up a desire of bloodshed in the
arms. Hypocrisy's head explodes and
crawl out countless bears, tame dogs,
bats and wild cats. Nobody has the spirit
of a warrior to stand this grim misfortune,
the all have turned into eunuchs,
mockers or scoundrels.

Intelligentsia has fallen into a
torpor.... narcosis snaps not. On artists
canvas lines shoot irregularly.... Picasso
echoes only in chats and in every town
artists jabber Piccasso and turning themselves
into clowns shuffle hither and thither. Drainpipe
trousers and the dappled shirts make no
paintings. There is a fire that has been
extinguished and in ashes have been buried
the trees of sensations and the germs of sensibility.

The third world war is before the eyes
and the whole continent keeps mum. Nobody
speaks nor makes a stir. Women do wait
but nobody turns to make love or debauch.
It is coincidence that torpor is snapped at
times and a red hand-bill is distributed
and people commemorating the back dates
wait for the noose ready for them.

Waiting is the whole truth and
the whole continent is bearing it. Rivers
are flowing endlessly--necromancers are
singing chants--some gorilla will jump
on a mutilated body and in his immense
paw will clutch all houses, machines, winds
and radars.

Cries will remain imprisoned in the
staring eyes and mankind will exist only
on the pages of history--posterity will
sing the chorus, is a fancy. They will
commemorate the past--it's all humbug. This
is to be her ultimate destiny. It's a fancy that
something will come about in this crippled country.

I will remain silent and unstirred
I won't perform any sacrifice
I won't string the bow
Suffering in a void
turning into a black stone of destiny
I am waiting silently for the doomsday:
sad and dull.

(Tr.: Ratan Chauhan)

Witness to a Dying History

A violent current of black blood rushes
on the left of my ribs. What remains is desire
of bloodshed and everything has been disfigured
and changed into a lie. Somebody has tarred
the faces of acquaintances and trees and
houses have been blown up with dynamite.

The feel of things has grown so faint that
what remains is the prick of spears in the
brain. A heavy swell has come over
the arms and legs and a splitting poison
in the eyes. To rest one's head on some
breast and sleep is mere sentimentality,
the next moment a double-barrelled gun will
be pointed at and the whole skull torn in
pieces will be scattered in the air.

What remains is a corpse that I have been
bearing for the last so many years. The fire
of the pen that scribbles between the trembling
fingers has been damped down. Picasso, who
wastes his time on abstract art is mad--
every face has been discoloured, every stroke
breaks in the centre of the head.
Some horrid creature is devouring man, colours
and time with the vibrations of brain.

The neck, I have been pining
for last so many years to see standing erect:
men have shoulders that don't know how
to be straight. Only silence reigns and a
poisonous snake that coils round the
waist of the people and strikes its hood

at the threshold. What remains is a prick
of lightnings in the eyes terrible and the
heat of age in the hair turned grey.

A small chameleon takes tiny bites sometimes
and scratches at the hair--only the skin
twitches and the thighs are straightened--
What remains is darkness, a black red-tongued
Bakasur opens his jaws and devours the
necks and the shoulders and the breasts.

Nobody bears a Witness to this dying history,
nobody puts in a claim for this debauchery.
This blind machinery and its eyes are
covered with a piece of red cloth and the
pictures of Ho-Chi-Minh hung round
the neck - only rotten onions and
outdated newspapers and corks of bottles are
lying on some streets.

In the whole country persons compete in
petty struggles. Having worn a hermit's pose
people have fallen in a yogi-like slumber.
Nobody wants a dapple-grey cat to snap
out of its sleep; nobody wants an encounter
on the frontiers or a procession of mad
dogs in the metropolis.

What remains is a wait for a clutch--
for some wolf's paws. That daring hero
may be anybody some revolutionary,
some hideous gorilla or the crown of
the detective stories--the Red Paw.

(Tr.: Ratan Chauhan)

A Poisonous Generation

The black rose
in my small garden
has withered and drooped,
the ever green Molsiri
Growing pale
has trickled.

I am sad today
Perhaps I have been shadowed
by some ghost
untraceable

A number of faces
of Innocence
are crawling round me -
clumsy faces,
faces pale and sad
whose eyes have swollen
and overflowing with pus.

Really
my aspirations
are drinking every crumb of air -
they are bulling on
drinking the arsenic of words
done in poison.

Comfort me
O, the great poisonous snake of furrow
Bite me not
curl up
your frothy venomous
tongues.

Your bite
won't kill me.
I am proof against poisons -
I have become a symbol
of mithridate.
I have lived my life
in the vicinity of thorns.
I won't die,
I have been reared up
by the poisonous-maidens.

I am sipping poison
taking it to be
a delicious drink,
my apathy towards
evils
has made me immune
to poison.

I shall go on living
and create a new world.
I am Brahma,
I shall start life anew
I shall luxuriate in
the flesh of poisonous maidens
and produce
a poisonous generation.

(Tr.: Ratan Chauhan)

Esctasy of Death

Depressed by a helpless grief
skeletons roam all about
continuously a scared crow
shrieks silently
under the colourless dwellings
of `pipal' tree.

A sound in gasping lane
echoes--
Tired dogs with covetous tongues
Vomit
a dead city through their saliva.

The whole dead city is smelling
of cooked meat, of legs, of hairs
of painted dolls akin to
unnatural poetry.

A blue river flows quietly amidst
the vast expanse of the city
Dogs and Vultures in the prayer houses
Engrossed in coitius, burn their limbs.

All alone I flow. Perhaps I knew to coverage
Floating quitely
I place my hand on dilapidated house
on the marble platform,
I murdered the city,
an unknown woman
And fled bewildered.

Throwing spirit on the houses
I set fire.

It is now ablaze. Each house is burning
Alongwith the crops, the body,
the chest and a pair of breasts.

I am happy today
I will dance and drink
wine-soaked in blood and fat.

(Tr.: Tara Tikku)

Definition of Poetry

Revolution is impossible through poetry. Of course you can use it to beat the air. During revolution, martyrs did poetry at the point of death for they spent the whole of life cleaning pistols in the jungles far from the world of poetry. Poetry is not a pistol that you pick it and break open the skull of the century.

I have prepared a definition of poetry. Cram it up if you like and get it distributed in the Departments of Hindi in the universities of India. It begins not in words, it is in the margin- the margin not on a piece of paper, it's that of a hat. And you know it well, when worn out of doors, a man looks smart. It displays grace. Its out-turned part strikes a note. Beyond the loose "Dhoti" and "Langots", poetry is now sitting on a hat. Eliot gives you a fright and Walt Whitman-you consider him exotic? Do you forget, Sir, that in our country, a thing like poetry for fifty years drew sighs from the dhoti-clad Babus and has drowned from pavements to pillows in bedrooms with tears?

Correct Sir ! This poetry deteriorates not. It holds a market. Girls are crazy about it. If you like, get it confirmed from some Miss College. You may see her humming a ghazal at a bus stop. You are getting bored these days. New poetry suits you not. You please take Vitamin tablets and rub perfumed oil for a year on your head.

Do not read Nietzche- you will go mad. You take poetry to be a sleeping pill. The words of Nietzche will advise you to drill a hole in the earth. Do not get frightened. He was a prodigy. Hitler was produced by what his pen scribbled. What a terror this Nazi was !

Were you born then ? This dictator shook the whole of Europe.

If you get frightened, give up talking this poetry business. Your wife must be looking for you. What makes you to stay here for the night so long? Don't you know this poetry gives you an illusion to kill you before time. All good poets died young.

Turning talks to death is not pleasant to your taste. But my good friend, this is a fact that poetry choses to come only through this bloody path and as being scribbled by few maniacs, it comes to trouble the sleep of people.

(Tr.: Ratan Chauhan)

City of Stones

After a long voyage, I stopped in a city of stones
only black sleepy rocks
and Boulders with outgrown noses existed.

Rock cliffs dashed my eyes in the dark
A dead-shadow kept wandering round me.

The sun never turned over here.
An iniquitous clarity of this horrifying darkness
threw a coarse blanket on my shoulders
And made holes in my vertebrae.

The air droned
A murderous cascade kept flowing
I couldn't tempt to peep into any safe-door.

Might not the sun turn up
Might not an evil spirit of a living being touch me.

I, filled with zeal,
Roamed desperately in dark caves.
The foul smell of a two legged mammal
Forced me to come here.

Human voices made me nauseous
The murderous motives behind friendliness
Made me terrified.

Love:
The ugly face of which I discovered
In the groaning of a monstrous ape.
In this non-humane magic world
I searched for a terrifying horror.

A bruised monster of terror
Made me to run with air
Through various cities
And made me a stranger
Amongst black yellow bodies
Familiar by their nation's name.

Books licked me like termites
And a sharp edged dagger
Kept hanging on my head.

I tried to give a name to this dark city
On its stony boundry, I endeavoured
To put some colourless cloth.

But flags witnessed blood only
And the hands uplifting them were
A friend of one
And a foe of the other.

On that deformed rock
Which looked like the skull of a horrifying man
Neither could I write a name
Nor any sign.

In that droning air
I silently witnessed:
The falling springs, eroding mountains
Merging valleys
the lessening of hair with aging
And
The diminishing brightness of the eye.

(Tr.: Yugank Chaturvedi)

Cave of Indecision

The sharp blows of lonely life
Severed my wings.

I struggle for breath
Like a wingless bird

Nothing in life....nowhere.....

All lines are tangled
In a distorted play of geometry
Where do I find straight lines ?

Living aimlessly
Like a lone tree on a mountain top
Shivering in frost.

Nobody knows when
A sudden storm will uproot it
Nobody knows.

Nothing is certain in life
I am rotting in a cave of
indecision.

(Tr.: Arun Sedwal)

Undecided

Suddenly, it seems,
the present has disappeared into a tunnel
all the relationships were a dark thick smoke
that had clouded the entire body and thought process.

I vow not to touch any familiar sign
I vow not to call any familiar name
under the sky there's filthy drain
I vow not to swim across.

A serpentine ritual is being performed in my spine quietly
some unknown hands are throwing out weapons
with poison drenched voices.

It is not necessary to search for signatures
in history
in order to disbelieve it.

Climbing on the hard seventh rock of the cycle of destiny
I've found my destination
the tongues shall not be able to lick the blood
gushing out to streams,
the entire sky shall go orphan
the two carrion-crows shall remain seated
in an undecided mood, over an unknown question.

The recurrent centuries shall vomit poison
in search of a new name
the perennial tree shall shed its leaves
on the trunk shall be notched a long name
dry and flat.

(Tr.: R.S. Yadav)

Revaluation

The blueness of the sky is destroyed
by the approach of dark, grotesque clouds.
The burning sun has disappeared
in the deep, unknown valleys.
Exhausted travellers have started again
in search of their path

An unknown time has passed in waiting
Nobody came
Neither the air changed nor its warmth!

Again, a clever voice started shattering my bones
Film-reels flashed in the thick darkness of the eyes
Dark green, injured snakes crawled on the beds
And beautiful nests of sparrows started falling
from huge, giant trees

You stick memories on the streets
Now their existence is submerged under the thick, black
`kottar'
The names on trees are being wrenched off by violent
currents
And on the park-benches
Where we embraced incessantly -
Leafless branches are leaning
Over those silent standing pine trees.

Air, light and dreams
How unreal is their perception !
With the passage of time
The eye too changes.

In the past what we considered
An eternal signature on the face of this age
Today, they have become faint
And from them are appearing
Limbs of ancient corpses
And symbols of faulty, weak lines of history.

One day history becomes an unreality
Memories get transformed into a diffused picture
of some Gorilla's skeleton
Or green algae on the dead pillars

Now day-break is a black sun
Eve is a drowned river of
stony, white mountains.

Memories are a pale city
In which
Only corpses live
And skulls burst into laughter
On the remaining: ruins of
a decaying culture.

(Tr.: Suresh Dhingra)

Truth of History

You consider beauty a dazzling fire
I deliberate it for a petty bird
You consider beauty an inspiration
I sheer wastage of time.

It was you
Who once declared it with confidence
that
Poetry changes a nation
And
Woman transforms history.

You stated it
And I didn't even utter a word
In my eye
Poetry and woman are immaterial
To history and society.

You listened to me
And lost your steadiness - my friend
The monstrous tradition of centuries
The rich heritage of culture
And
The humane values of life
Made you sad and worried.

Then, you blamed me
I tolerated that
you abused me
I remained silent.

You came to me after years
Sad, firm and worried as usual

In an attempt to speak
You came closer to my ears

You seemed to have passed these days in agony
You must have madly gone through the books
You seemed to have already sipped
a lot of life poison
The wrinkles on the face approved it.

You murmered softly
I was astonished
You were saying----
Poetry made me aloof of self
And
Woman separated me from kin.

(Tr.: Yugank Chaturvedi)

The Generation of Idles

All of us are bored
Tired of this routine
Grinded under its hateful iron wheel.

We are all prisoners
Poor innocent animals
Imprisoned for life in some jail.

Like a vulture sitting on the broken bridge
We are waiting for the time--
We are all unsuccessful, spiritless,
insipid children--
of a generation
That relies on destiny--
The wheel of fortune.

The songs on piano do not please us
The people sitting on the cushions fret us
Full of our own selfish motives
We spread abuses over others.

We are all scarabs decaying in death
Whose growth has ceased
We are all beetles and mosquitoes
Of stagnant water of a dead pool
Our generation is a generation of parasites, lethargics.

The only difference between us and the oilman's ox
Is that
We find nothing out of our endeavour
And he--
gets his definite result
By dragging on a defined track.

(Tr.: Arun Sedwal)

Excess of Hatred

Last morning
The aged face of the sun
Seemed a little tilted.

And the wings of the butterflies
Crawling on the green lawn
Seemed frozen.
(Though it had not snowed)

I suddenly realised
That to have loved you was
My biggest blunder.

In the mirror
I found a dog's face staring at me
Instead of my own
And the portrait kept in my desk drawer
And the ink spilled on the chip-floor
Seemed so akin to my face.

The day's love-
What a marvellous deception
on all fours.

A God-made blasted world
of grotesque colours,
where to hate others
Is to hate myself the more.

(Tr.: Arun Sedwal)

The Will

He has thought of making a will.

He will record names of all those
Who landed him money
Or borrowed from him

He will record sizes of blouses
Of all those women
Who slept with him
And of those who fled
With fear taking excuse
Through bath room doors
To their husbands or fathers
To seek refuge.

He wants to build a house
Without the staircase
He feels pain climbing up
His ankles ache
And his pregnant beloveds
Could abort while going up.

He will not mention anyone ladder like.
Be it a bureaucrat
Or an insurance agent
or a famous advocate
Or a future teller.

He is sorry for it would not be possible
To mention his father's name.
He has been weak at mathematics
But he knows
His father's strong can walk for days.

He is fearsome of the approaching day-the day of Death
Whence his father chews canes
and brushes the teeth
with bitter Indian stick

He'll definitely mention in the Will
His friend Narendra Dhir
Whose teeth fell at thirty two - the tender age
And whose face turned at forty
to that of a spoilt monarch of seven and half decades.

He is not joking. He remembers fine
Parrots or Ravindra Kalia at times!

But Kali never eats *Sattu*
And he keeps with him digestives all the times.
If he mentions digestives in his Will
Abbot Veerumal would object.
He withdraws the name of this disease!

He went to Ootty last summer
He couldn't get wine there
The rains were heavy
He kept remembering Rajkamal Chaudhary
To weather he called names.

He likes guitar by Van Shipley
But wants to play Piano.
But his beloved doesn't know
How to dance.
She writes verses
Or sad she remains.
He doesn't want to remember
A sad damsel in the moment
When by death he is slain.

He had met a girl
In Park Street, Calcutta
Harnam opined
She was next to none.
He never conscribed with this
But he wants
To make the heir apparent
Of his last wealth
That Japanese girl
Un-named to mind.

How dearly he wanted to visit Japan.
He feels many a time
He went to homes and coffee houses
of Tokyo.
He feels many a night
He spent with geisha girls.
They are not flabby like the Bengali ones.
He wants to belt-tie a cloth
And get into a Japanese ship.

He wants to distribute his wealth
To all the begging litterateurs
Of undeveloped nations
Who think their cross roads
As 'Greenwich village'
And talk of 'Happening'
to their pregnant wives.

He is angry with Soumitra Mohan
For he couldn't find
'Lukman Ali' till his death
If him he could find
That homo would have bought himself
Stuffed brinjals and gravied vegetables.

Now as he prepares to depart
His fingers shiver.
His buttons can't hold the pant intact
He is willing himself everything
So that no one makes a waving act
So that they concede he was father of Kabir
After his death.

(Tr.: Suresh Dhingra)

A Perception

Early in the morning
Yesterday
A little bird breathed its last.

Queer were those wet little eyes.

I feel as if
In a distant country
Many miles away
My little daughter lies restless on the death-bed,
I would see her never-never.

(Tr.: Anamika)

Tea House

Tea-House is a crematoria
Where we mourn formally
And receive the joys of the grave.

At night no sleep.

(Tr.: Arun Sedwal)

Conversation

In the tranquility of the street
Stand
Three Banyan trees

As if
Talking
They bend towards each other.

(Tr.: Maneesha Upadhyaya)

Birth of A Child

Yesterday night two trees
grew in me-
Cactus and rose

Two infant hands
Knocked the door.

(Tr.: Prabhakar Machwe)

Death

Last night two dogs died
One male, the other female-
Hungry like us
For centuries.

(Tr.: Arun Sedwal)

Progress

The world has gone ahead

The girl
Who until yesterday
Would pirouette before me naked
Has eloped
With a coolie.

(Tr.: Arun Sedwal)

Inconsistant

When I look at young women
I grin;
Feel their breasts in my palms
Make a fond image in my mind
Of their groins, ribs and naked arms.

But when a woman
Smiles at me
I feel my limbs melting
And becoming impotent.

(Tr.: Maneesha Upadhyaya)

Literary Teacher

You gave me a lesson in love
Oh! innocent girl, you are my teacher!

Even if you hadn't been there
It would have made no such difference
Instead of creating poetry
I would have been found
in a grocer's shop,
weighing salt.

(Tr.: Arun Sedwal)

Quest for the Unknown

I don't know
when this giant demon may stretch
its sinister hands of hatred
and transform himself
from a stone icon into a living being.

My veins are unable to differentiate
which venom is meant for life
and which one for death
(Perhaps it is a physician's job to know)

To seek the essence of life
I entangled myself with books / universe/
God and the maxims of *Kathopanishad*

One night emerging from the darkness
a thousand-winged adjutant
snatched away my brain
an owl wiped out eyes from my face.

Noise, revenge--
-- was no more on my blank face
God incarnated Himself
and entered into my tissues

In my living hands, I held a dead face
carved by dexterous hands
I saw it without my eyes
and even with no nose
I felt its fragrance

Holding a body in my hands
I sat motionless

and was solving the mysteries of--
sky, darkness and of human reminiscences

Labyrinth of memories--
spread out in the valley like a fisherman's net
the air was filled only with the odour of fishes
the sky was in my hands
and the eyes had come back into my sockets
with a new light.

finding some fireflies on my palms
I felt God:
red, yellow lines gliding in the infinite bluish sky
--a fragmented rainbow.

And then a wounded dream--
crying with pain--
lay near my feet.

I felt truth is neither hatred nor love
Truth is only *Being*
which does not live or die
it only creates vibrations in some bodies
some chunks of earth quiver

and in the pervasive silence of cremation-ground
sits a love-incarnated saintly man
under the waning moon
in the posture of submission
and remembers Him.

(Tr.: Krishna Ashant)

Dots, No Lines

Tree trunks shuddering in the tides of winds,
the foundations of megapolis too are seized
as though by an acute ague

Someone writes, rewrites someone's name
throughout a long night,
and lets it slip out of mind as day breaks

She sits solitary, glance fixed on ground below-
passes by on a path buried under
a scattering of shrivelling leaves

Sunlight sprawls silently, as parash dogs rear
on their haunches and rail at tall mansions
in fits of endless tedious debate

I pick up a burnt out cigar off the pavement
and placing my head on my knees
relight it to a semblance of life

A cold breath descends from the dome of an empty sky
and no matter which way, from it away I back
it instantaneously makes its monotonous message heard

Foxily the night escapes in stealth into dense foliage,
while beneath my skin is felt the stinging
of a hundred needles of finest point.

In desolation meandering a fugitive shadow is observed
impatient as if to submit,
to human bondage

The sky parts:
at once its big mouth spits out
a shower of incandescent sparks

And now, I dig my toes in my threadbare shoes and plod
towards alleys in whose pervasive dark-
not long past-I would not have been caught dead.

(Tr.: Keshav Malik)

The Broken 'I'

In the midst of uncertainty I live on like a lamentation.

My ego---
a crow in repentance
that hovers around the peepal like a ghost, the whole life
keeps on pecking me in my entrails.
And in the feathers of this torture are hideously hidden
snakes of the machine age!

The snakes have bruised all crops:
people are dying like tapeworms
and crowing like the cocks, chased in their helplessness.

And I --
a pigeon whose feathers have been clipped
keep on fluttering around
helpless, hopeless
in the cell that smacks of the disabled vampirebats!

The suffocation of uncertainty
vomits larvae
like small white eggs of tortoises
and the scavengers veiled in dark thin shrouds
strut on the naked bodies of women, all of them!

Among those who are living
are oysters, mosquitoes and scavengers
and, of course, the litters of lizards;
all the intellectuals are sad
either mute or restive
like the frightened young ones of sparrows!

A trunk apart from head and limbs,

I am lying idle
dying slowly;
the snakes creep around
in the city of these wood pieces, scavengers and demons
and the dead bodies laugh ha...ha...
My uncertainty
like a person just now entombed alive
struggles and struggles...but all in vain
and accepts the earthen shroud!

In the earthen shroud
I feel a sense of certainty;
I smile
and squeeze to death ant lying there
and turn to the blind alley of death, last of all.

(Tr.: Motilal Jotwani)

Subconscious: A Flash

The sigh of the night
has found a shelter to sleep
in the exhausted eyes of owls.
The owls--indulged in copulation

A deadly silence prevails around
All the ant-hills are asleep--
But--
to bite me, the snakes--
(On yes! the hissing snakes)
--are creeping...creeping towards me.

And my mind--
like shadow of a crawling respiration
squeezes itself--
in a weaver bird's nest
on the silent tamarind tree--
shrouded with hazy rays of the Moonshine

(Tr.: Krishna Ashant)

Detachment

I have cut myself from the past ruthlessly.

Nothing could be seen except claws of a ferocious cat
Marks of a few scratchings
Left on the body.

A cloud of flesh sometimes emerging
from the left
obstructs the respiration of the wind-pipe.

I stuffed some papers in the vacant place
At a time, I was interested in these
Guarded them as treasures.

I stopped passing through a shivering villa
Sometimes a shrill voice obstructs the way
A few scared rabbits jump out of my pocket
Start dancing under the street light.

I know the futility of
Light, wind and expectation.

I have returned from a long journey
And hidden the carcasses of beloveds
In the bogies of the train
And I have fled.

(Tr. Tara Tikku)

The Solitude Shatters

Your face is dejected
But eyes have an unfathomable charm
in your quietness
swims the longings to bind the sky

Your utterances
Make the seasons talk
Your sweet smiles
arouse the sleeping laurels

Why have you thought seclusion a feeble thing
when the Solitude shatters
The shadows of Adam in their soothing shades
cover the sky
the grandeur of nature

And in an quizzical sleep
merges the spirit
Hereafter the contented caresses.

(Tr. Maneesha Upadhyaya)

Loneliness Breaks

Your face is sad
But there is an unending hypnotism in your eyes
In your muteness
Floats a craving to limit the sky.

When you speak
The seasons speak
When you laugh
The garden awakes.

Why do you take solitude to be helpless
When loneliness breaks
Primitive shadows cover the sky,
Nature's riches-
In their cool shade.

And in an unbelievable sleep-
The body sinks
After intimate embraces.

(Tr.: Maneesha Upadhyaya)

Four Love Poems

For Beloved No. 1 (I)

Your were a sky as fresh and bright as snow
And you over-shadowed me
And the little thicked in me
In toto

Yes, you were my mother, darling!

For Beloved No. 2 (S)

Beyond all relationships
I fell for your eyes
You touched me with the fragrance
of your limbs
You were autumnal horizon:
Moon lit

You irrigated the soil of my soul,
dearest!

For Beloved No. 3 (R)

You were my love,
I loved you with the utmost passion
I would have remained
As innocent as dove-
Had you not given me
Your cosy lap of leaves:
You were the light of my limbs-
Really!

For Beloved No. (K).

You were much much younger to me
But when I saw you
Roses blossomed in my blood-
Green and blue and yellow.

On your palms was engraved my future,
You were my prospect, dearest!

(Tr. Anamika)

Music of the Malwa

His passion for the past has not yet faded.

Those dusty hills and the parrot-borne forests
Are yet alive as ever in his eyes.
He is still locked-up in the greenery
Of nature, the riches of his innocent childhood.
The maulsiri trees, the aging banyan
And the cool winds aloft acacia
Baring its glow on his cheeks.

His heart turns an ascetic wanderer
And wearing Saffron robes
Craves to flee to the forests
Where there are no asphyxiating smokes
No cement jungles, flintlike men
Nor voices croaking in snobbery....

He and the black deer
Lotus bloomed ponds
And a large pandanus flower
To attract in his fond childish kinship
With its glow, white and purple
Assimilating the sunset in his eyes.

Such love and attraction
As the asset of Malwa soil
And to know scores of fresh flowers
Yet locked in his heart, is to know oneself
The first awareness of self-understanding
Amongst all trivialities.

yes, I do believe
On those rocky hill tops.

Cherubs float, not clouds.
A morose child gazes at reflections bright
And jumps down to swim across
The sour kshipra river.

A tiny butterfly-wing
Chases him on and on
And an empty sky pours down
In his eye-lids

In his eyes keep floating
The green fields of Malwa
And the water maids
In attire colourful,
And in his views
Bloossoms a lotus
From shrines of Kalidasa.

The golden crops
In the soil black,
The moon in the sky,
Bewitching nights
And a smile twinkling, tender
By the dolls house
Beneath the banyan tree

Some planets shiver
In his eyes
And Lord Shiva
In the mighty posture of
Mahakaleshwar
Freezes down before him
Annoucing the great halt of mighty Nandi

A huge giant waves his tongue
Before him,
He feels the demon of Death
So close to him
In the Tantrapeetha
The red eyes of stray dogs
Wake him up.

He is fond of Akshayvata
The waves of Kshipra revolving round the Mars,
A flute of Krishna cooing in his thicket,
A song wakes up in his blood.

Sandeepini ashram surrounds it
And the peace that
Are there very much.
But where are gone
Lord Shri Krishna and
The great force of
Comradeship of oneself
That flows and overflows
And overcomes Sudama's miseries.

The lanes of Ujjain
Still have the foot-prints
Of Kalidasa's fair maids
And flower-shrines,
A fragrance rare
And a whole tradition
of ascetics in silk attires feeding
On the rare plantain leaves

Bharathari's cave,
Kapaliks shrine
And the weird postures
Of intoxicant hermits.

O so dear-dear-dear
Is this township,
So dear-dear-dear
Are nights.
They have been pets of
Bajbahadur, Roopmati
And wolfish marauders of Gujarat

The history bears an evidence to the fact
That lotuses blossom in its ponds,
No one starves
The soil fragrant and fertile
Echoes with the ringle-tingle of
The little fairy queens.

Kshipra river drives him crazy even now
On banks of the old banyan trees
Two little palms joined together
To scratch out names.
In the cool bewilderness of
caves in haunted forests
Twinkle fire-flies of memories.

A seedling tender
Of charm undefined.
Raised its head
From deep down
The soil black
In the manner of a fountain
That breaks through the rock.

Sometimes he feels
That peace blossoms
Only when amidst all noise
There are smiles fragrance in the wood of memoirs,
which drive you to a very rare trance.

Journeys, Journeys through the clouds
On the bullock-carts.

In dark-lamp pre-independence days serene
were lighted some kerosene lamps
By some shaky hands
That could climb up and up
like magic men
On bambooes stem.

The buses blue
Men in turbans,
Maids in jewellery fake and bright
Working in the fields!
Trees running on and on
Yelling dogs on bullocks.

Haunted river of Shajapur,
Mini, temporary markets,
Old school,
Stuffy room of the headmaster
Where Maharaja Jivaji Rao Scindia smiled
In diamonds, turbans and pearls,
In a frame!

In Independence movement
Nights stole all sleep
From the great eyes of the sky red:
blood red!

The map of the country

stepped in his veins:
The Punjab and Kashmir
The throbbing feet of cyclone
And the roaring ocean great!

In the dawn of Independence
Shivpuri was a little summer capital
With fountains and many a rocky hills,
Roads red and countless seasames,
Fragrant parks with peacocks,
Squirrels teasing everyone
With little tongues out.

In ecstasy,
Deer black and
Raindeer with off-innocent eyes!
Owls old shrieking hard
On haunted branches!

The sun of his adolescence
Stood numb on Western horizon
He could say body from body
And colour from colour
And the poetry of looks
Meant something for him,
Dreams danced hazily,
Drowsily in blood!

The first kiss dew-soft
On the petal-soft bushes
of her hair
Dense and wet
Under darkening sky!
O Two bewitching eyes:
Wide and deep!

Rainbows blossomed on hill tops,
Over oceans of the light
In the mornings as bright
As cotton-flowers!
Thousand pearls from fountains / falls
All assembled.

A flute called him passionately,
In notes deep,
From behind the valleys
Where roamed tribes,
Beasts ferocious!

There were many little hunters around
In his troop,
But he deserted them all
When he noticed someone dead:
Fleeing deer and
Raindeer all pleaded for mercy.

And that triangular bungalow
With a pair of those
Soft and thirsty,
Peepy, seepy eyes
On the window pane!

How he grew up with them
Within the flames rising high
In his blood
On the grass very green
Malwa means so much,
The mountains of Shivpuri sing a melodious note,
He quarrels with himself,
On the roads zig zag and red.

Journeys can be both pleasant
And torturous he knows.
The road to adolescence
was paved with such agonies!
Waiting and waiting
And waiting till death.
Time : It can't be arrested,
O, can it be?

The dust on the road
Goes straight to the eyes
To give acute pinches,
The lotus in palms fades away,
fades away,
fades away!

This is the love saga
Of the dancing maids
swift as wind in the wood.
And so fresh!
He is the nomad lover in the tale.

He feels the fragrance of soil
Breathes through him
And when two smiles meet
A strong impulse
Dances fast
On the earth
Like the cyclone.
Where two currents cross
And meet and fall together,
A temple is raised.

The long worshipped rock in the temple
Still throbs in his veins
And he knows not
How deep rooted is this
Gravitational pull
That binds him
with those sounds,
With that soil:

The land of lyrics,
The music of Malwa.

(Tr.: Anamika)

[illegible]

The long worship of rocks in the temple
Still thickens his veins
And he knows not
How deep rooted is this
Gravitational pull
That binds time
Within our sounds
With that soil

The land of lyrics
The music of Marwar.

[illegible]

Nirala Series

Nepal, Bhutan, South Asia and Himalayan Studies

Maoists in the Land of Buddha
An Analytical Study of the Maoist Insurgency in Nepal
Prakash A. Raj
ISBN 81-85693-42-0 2004 Hard pp.210

The Yeti
Spirit of Himalayan Forest Shamans
Larry G. Peters
ISBN 81-85693-57-9 2004 Hard pp.224

Rana Rule in Nepal
Saphalya Amatya
ISBN 81-85693-67-6 2004 Hard pp.392

Trance, Initiation & Psychotherapy in Nepalese Shamanism
Essays on Tamang and Tibetan Shamanism
Larry G. Peters
ISBN 81-85693-79-X 2004 Hard pp.412

The Gurkha Connection
A History of Gurkha Recruitment in the British Army
Purushottam Baskota
ISBN 81-85693-77-3 2004 Paper pp.221

Dolpo : The Hidden Paradise
A Journey to the Endangered Sanctuary of the Himalayan Kingdom of Nepal
Karna Sakya
ISBN 81-85693-170-0 2004 Paper pp.246

Malla Coins of Medieval Nepal
Jagdish Chandra Regmi
ISBN 81-85693-60-9 2004 Hard

The Questions of Dharma in the Mahabharata
Birendra Mishra
ISBN 81-85693-48-X 2004 Hard pp.226

Popular Deities, Emblems and Images of Nepal
Dhruba K. Deep
With a 'Foreword' by Lain S. Bangdel
ISBN 81-85693-39-0 2003 Paper pp.180

The Gurungs : Thunder of Himal
A Cross-cultural Study of a Nepalese Ethnic Group
Murari P. Regmi
ISBN 81-85693-49-8 2002 Paper pp.238

The Gurkhas
A History of the Recruitment in the British Indian Army
Kamal Raj Singh Rathaur
ISBN 81-85693-85-4 2000 pp.128

The Political Economy of Land, Landlessness and Migration in Nepal
Nanda R. Shrestha
ISBN 81-85693-87-0 2001 Hard pp.309

Tourism in Nepal : Marketing Challenges
Hari Prasad Shrestha
With a 'Foreword' by Deependra Purush Dhakal
ISBN 81-85693-69-2 2000 Hard pp.400

Ethnic Conflict in Bhutan
Political and Economic Dimensions
Mathew Joseph C.
ISBN 81-85693-68-4 1999 Hard pp.251

Mountain Dimensions
An Altitude Geographic Analysis of Environment and Development of the Himalayas
Ram Kumar Pandey
ISBN-81-85693-43-9 1999 pp.260 Hard

Tamang Shamans
An Ethnopsychiatric Study of Ecstasy and Healing in Nepal
Larry G. Peters
With a 'Foreword' by Jacques Maquet
ISBN 81-85693-65-X 1999 Hard pp.179

Wildlife in Nepal
Rishikesh Shaha & Richard M.Mitchell
With Colour Plates by Nanda Shumsher J.B. Rana
ISBN 81-85693-31-5 2001 Paper pp.142

Nepal : Missing Elements

in the Development Thinking
Gunanidhi Sharma
ISBN 81-85693-66-8 2000 Hard pp.214

Making of Modern Nepal
A Study of History, Art and Culture of the Principalities of Western Nepal
Ram Niwas Pandey
ISBN 81-85693-37-4 1997 Hard pp.816

Art and Culture of Nepal
An Attempt towards Preservation
Saphalya Amatya
ISBN 81-85693-63-3 1999 Paper pp.282

Vishvarupa Mandir
A Study of Changu Narayan, Nepal's most Ancient Temple
Jeff Lidke
With a 'Foreword' by ***Ronald M. Bernier***
ISBN 81-85693-59-3 1996 Hard. pp.213

Religious Minorities in Nepal
An Analysis of the State of Buddhist and Muslims in the Himalayan Kingdom
Mollica Dastider
ISBN 81-85693-47-1 1996 Hard pp.126

Human Rights in the Hindu-Buddhist Traditions
Lal Deosa Rai
ISBN 81-85693-46-3 1995 Hard pp.188

Fire of Himal
An Anthropological Study of the Sherpas of Nepal Himalayan Region
Ramesh Raj Kunwar
ISBN 81-85693-64-1 1999 Paper pp.314

The Khasa Kingdom
A Trans-Himalayan Empire of the Middle Age
Surya Mani Adhikary
ISBN 81-85693-50-1 1997 Paper pp.215

Nepal : A Concise History of the Cultural Scenario of the Himalayan Kingdom
Jagdish Shumsher Rana
ISBN 81-85693-45-5 1995 Hard pp.120

Bhutan : A Movement in Exile
D.N.S. Dhakal & Christopher Strawn
ISBN 81-85693-41-2 1994 Hard pp.639

Encounter Wildlife in Nepal
Karna Sakya
With a 'Foreword' by ***Harka Gurung***
ISBN 81-85693-38-2 1996 Hard pp.296

Nepal-India
Democracy in the Making of Mutual Trust
Dinesh Bhattarai & Pradeep Khatiwada
ISBN 81-85693-36-6 1993 Hard pp.324

Politics of Himalayan River Water
An Analysis of the River Water Issues of Nepal, India and Bangladesh
B.C. Uprety
With a 'Foreword' by ***Prof. Ramakant***
ISBN 81-85693-32-3 1993 Hard pp.228

The Himalayan Mind
A Cross-Cultural Nepalese Investigation
Murari P. Regmi
ISBN 81-85693-29-3 1994 Hard pp.240

Kathmandu, Patan & Bhakatpur
An Archaeological Anthropology of the Royal Cities of the Kathmandu Valley
Rishikeshab R. Regmi
ISBN 81-85693-30-7 1997 pp.111 Paper

A Glossary of Himalayan Buddhism
Jagadish Chandra Regmi
ISBN 81-85693-28-5 1994 Hard pp.212

The Nepala-Mahatmya
Legends on the Sacred Places and Deities of Nepal
Jayaraj Acharya
ISBN-81-85693-27-7 1992 Hard pp.320

Cultural Heritage of Nepal Terai
Ram Dayal Rakesh
ISBN 81-85693-26-9 1994 Hard pp.240

The Nepali Congress
An Analysis of the Party's Performance in the General Elections and its Aftermath
B.C. Uprety
ISBN 81-85693-33-1 1993 Hard pp.203

Recent Nepal
The Analysis of the Recent Democratic Upsurge and its Aftermath
Laksman Bahadur K.C.
ISBN 81-85693-24-2 1993 Hard pp.242

Politics and Development in Nepal :
Some Issues
Narayan Khadka
ISBN 81-85693-21-8 1994 Hard pp.477

Indo-Nepal Trade Relations
A Historical Analysis of Nepal's Trade with the British India
Shri Ram Upadhyaya
ISBN 81-85693-20-X 1992 pp.287

Politics and Development in Nepal :
Some Issues
Narayan Khadka
ISBN 81-85693-21-8 1994 Hard pp.477

Gods and Mountains
The Folk Culture of the Himalayan Kingdom of Nepal
Kesar Lall
ISBN 81-85693 1991 Hard pp.176

Folk Tales of Sherpa and Yeti
Shiva Dhakal
ISBN 81-85693-58-7 1996 pp.96

Hindu-Buddhist Festivals of Nepal
Hemanta Kumar Jha
ISBN 81-85693-40-4 1996 Hard pp. 117

Folktales from Mithila
Ram Dayal Rakesh
ISBN 81-85693-55-2 1996 Hard pp.126

Secrets of Shangri-La
An Inquiry into the Lore, Legend and Culture of Nepal
Nagendra Sharma
With a 'Foreword' by ***John Fredrick***
ISBN 81-85693-18-8 1992 pp.292

The Taming of Tibet
A Historical Account of Compromise and Confrontation in Nepal-Tibet Relations (1900-1930)
Tirtha Prasad Mishra
ISBN 81-85693-16-1 1991 pp.324

Glimpses of Tourism, Airlines and Management in Nepal
B.R. Singh
ISBN 81-85693-15-3 1991 pp.128

Sales Promotion in Nepal
Policies and Practices
Parashar Prasad Koirala
ISBN 81-85693-14-5 1991 pp.196

The Dhimals : Miraculous Migrants of Himal
An Anthropological Study of a Nepalese Ethnic Group
Rishikeshab Raj Regmi
ISBN 81-85693-13-7 1991 pp.269

Transit of Land Locked Countries and Nepal
Gajendra Mani Pradhan
ISBN 81-85693-08-0 1990 pp.240

Fundamentals of Library and Information Science
A Nepalese Response
Madhusudan Sharma Subedi
ISBN 81-85693-07-4 1990 pp.229

Folk Culture of Nepal
An Analytical Study
Ram Dayal Rakesh
With a 'Foreword' by ***Hiroshi Ishii***
ISBN 81-85693-06-4 1990 pp.129

A Macro-economic Study of the Nepalese Plan Performance
Gunanidhi Sharma
ISBN 81-85693-06-4 1989 pp.129

Sources of Inflation in Asia
Theory and Evidences
Raghab D. Pant
ISBN 81-85693-03-X 1988 pp.118

New Directions in Nepal - India Relations
Rishikesh Shaha
ISBN 81-85693-53-6 1995 Paper pp.64 Rs.65

In Nepali Language

Pashushala (Animal Farm)
(A Novel)
Georege Orwell
Translated from the English by **Bijuli Prasad Kayast**
ISBN 81-8250-000-1 2004 Paper pp.96

Nepalko Prajatantrik Andolan Ko Itihas
Surya Mani Adhikary
ISBN 81-85693-54-4 1998 Paper pp.468

Geetanjali (Nepali)
Rabindra Nath Tagore
Translated from the Bengali by **Ramesh Bhatta & Pashupati Neopane**
ISBN 81-85693-83-8 2000 Paper pp.125

Sarpahoru Geet Sundainan
Poems by **Shailendra Sakar**
With a 'Foreword' by Krishna Chandra Singh
ISBN 81-85693-98-6 1991 Hard pp.108

Anyatha Ashyiaya
Poems by **Shiva Adhikary**
With a 'Foreword' by Mohan Koirala
ISBN 81-85693-51-X 2001 Paper

U Bhaira Mero Abhiviakti
Poems by **Narendra Bahadur Shrestha**
With a 'Foreword' by Tara Nath Sharma
ISBN 81-85693-98-6 1989 Hard pp.112 Rs.60